3

BABIES AT THE ZOO
Polar Bear Cubs

Susan H. Gray

CHERRY LAKE PRESS

Published in the United States of America by
Cherry Lake Publishing
2395 South Huron Parkway, Suite 200, Ann Arbor, MI 48104
www.cherrylakepublishing.com

Content Advisor: Dominique A. Didier, Professor of Biology, Millersville University
Reading Advisor: Marla Conn, MS, Ed, Literacy specialist, Read-Ability, Inc.

Photo credits: ©Vladimir Wrangel/Shutterstock.com, front cover; ©outdoorsman/
Shutterstock.com, 1, 2; ©mycteria/Shutterstock.com, 4; ©Fotokon/
Shutterstock.com, 6; ©Belovodchenko Anton/Shutterstock.com, 8, 10, 16;
©MaruokaJoe/Shutterstock.com, 12; ©y.n/Shutterstock.com, 14; ©Sergey
Gerashchenko/Shutterstock.com, 18; ©olga_gl/Shutterstock.com, 20

Library of Congress Cataloging-in-Publication Data

Names: Gray, Susan Heinrichs, author.
Title: Polar bear cubs / written by Susan H. Gray.
Description: Ann Arbor, Michigan : Cherry Lake Publishing, 2020. |
    Series: Babies at the zoo | Includes index. | Audience: Grades K-1.
Summary: "Read about how polar bear cubs grow to be the biggest bear in
    the world and how zookeepers take care of them. This level 3 guided reader
    book includes intriguing facts and adorable photos. Students will develop
    word recognition and reading skills while learning about how these baby
    animals learn and grow, what they eat, and how they socialize with each
    other. Book includes table of contents, glossary, index, author biographies,
    sidebars, and word list for home and school connection"—Provided by
    publisher.
Identifiers: LCCN 2019034098 (print) | LCCN 2019034099 (ebook) |
    ISBN 9781534158962 (hardcover) | ISBN 9781534161269 (paperback) |
    ISBN 9781534160118 (pdf) | ISBN 9781534162419 (ebook)
Subjects: LCSH: Polar bear—Infancy—Juvenile literature. | Zoo animals—
    Infancy—Juvenile literature.
Classification: LCC SF408.6.P64 G735 2020 (print) | LCC SF408.6.P64 (ebook) |
    DDC 599.786—dc23
LC record available at https://lccn.loc.gov/2019034098
LC ebook record available at https://lccn.loc.gov/2019034099

Cherry Lake Publishing would like to acknowledge the work of the Partnership
for 21st Century Learning, a Network of Battelle for Kids. Please visit
http://www.battelleforkids.org/networks/p21 for more information.

Printed in the United States of America
Corporate Graphics

Table of Contents

About the Author

Susan H. Gray has a master's degree in zoology. She has written more than 150 reference books for children and especially loves writing about animals. Susan lives in Cabot, Arkansas, with her husband, Michael, and many pets.

Why are big feet good in the snow?

Mothers and Babies

What is the biggest bear in the world? The **polar** bear! Polar bears are large, furry **mammals**. They live near cold, **Arctic** seas. Some polar bears live in zoos.

Polar bears are made for the Arctic. Thick fur keeps them warm. Wide feet are good for walking on snow. Strong legs are good for swimming.

Baby bears are called cubs. Mothers usually have **twin** cubs. At birth, they have short, thin fur. Their eyes are closed. They cannot walk around.

The mother bear has her babies in a **den**. It is safer and warmer than being outside. The babies snuggle with their mom. They drink her milk.

At the Zoo

Zookeepers make sure polar bears stay healthy. They weigh the cubs. They also check the bears' teeth and claws.

Would you share your swimming pool with a polar bear?

Zookeepers want the bears to feel at home. So they bring in loads of snow. They keep the place cold. They even bring little swimming pools for the cubs.

Growing Up

Cubs stay inside the den for their first few months. Their fur grows soft and fluffy. Their eyes open. They begin to explore the den.

Babies stay with their mom for about 30 months. Their mother teaches them to hunt. The cubs stop drinking milk. Now they eat meat and fish.

Polar bears are adults at about 6 years. Then it is time to have cubs of their own.

Little babies are so cute and furry!

Find Out More

BOOK

Newman, Mark. *Polar Bears.* New York, NY: Square Fish, 2015.

WEBSITE

San Diego Zoo—Polar Bears Play in Snow
https://kids.sandiegozoo.org/videos/polar-bears-play-snow
Learn more about polar bears by watching a video of them
  playing in the snow.

Glossary

Arctic (ARK-tik) the area around the North Pole

den (DEN) a shelter for a wild animal

explore (ik-SPLOR) to travel and look around in order to
  discover things

mammals (MAM-uhlz) animals that have hair and provide
  milk to their babies

polar (POH-lur) near the North or South Pole

snuggle (SNUHG-uhl) to stay close to keep warm or safe

twin (TWIN) one of two babies born at the same time to the
  same mother

zookeepers (ZOO-kee-purz) people who take care of zoo animals

Home and School Connection

Use this list of words from the book to help your child become a better reader. Word games and writing activities can help beginning readers reinforce literacy skills.

a	claws	growing	meat	snuggle	up
about	closed	grows	milk	so	usually
adults	cold	has	mom	soft	walk
also	cubs	have	months	some	walking
and	cute	healthy	mother	stay	want
arctic	den	her	mothers	stop	warm
are	drink	home	near	strong	warmer
around	drinking	hunt	now	sure	weigh
at	eat	in	of	swimming	what
babies	even	inside	on	teaches	why
baby	explore	is	open	teeth	wide
bear	eyes	it	outside	than	with
bears	feel	keep	own	the	world
begin	feet	keeps	place	their	would
being	few	large	polar	them	years
big	first	legs	pool	then	you
biggest	fish	little	pools	they	your
birth	fluffy	live	safer	thick	zoo
bring	for	loads	seas	thin	zookeepers
called	fur	made	share	time	zoos
cannot	furry	make	short	to	
check	good	mammals	snow	twin	

Fast Facts

Habitat: Arctic sea ice, tundra, and coasts

Range: Far northern polar regions of North America, Europe, and Russia

Average Height: 6 to 8 feet (2 to 2.5 meters). Large males can be 13 feet (4 meters) tall.

Average Weight: 331 to 1,764 pounds (150 to 800 kilograms)

Life Span: 30 years

Anatomy: Polar bear skin is actually black.

Behavior: Polar bears are excellent swimmers.

Index